WonderWorks

Decodable Reader

Unit 3

Mc
Graw
Hill

Contents

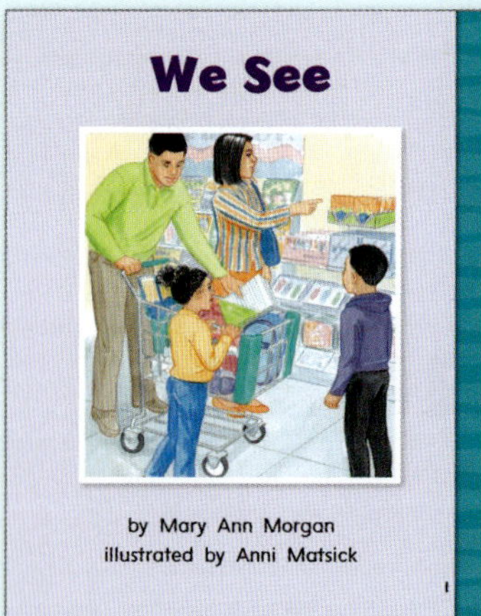
We See
by Mary Ann Morgan
illustrated by Anni Matsick
1

We Like to See
by Amy Kent
illustrated by Anthony Accardo
9

Nat and the Nap
by Tamira Johnson
illustrated by Gary Undercuffler
17

We See

by Mary Ann Morgan
illustrated by Anni Matsick

Sam can **see** **the**  .

pencils

Pat can **see** **the**  .

paper

We can **see** **the**  .

crayons

We can **see** **the** 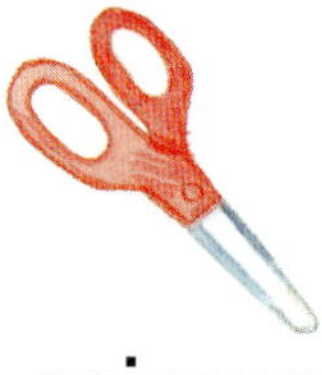.
scissors

Pat can **see** **the**  .

paste

We can **see** **the**  .

money

We Like to See

by Amy Kent

illustrated by Anthony Accardo

Tim can see the  .

van

We like **to** see the 

.

stop sign

We like **to** see the  .

pig

We like **to** see the  .

truck

We like **to** see the  .

bike

We like **to** see  !

Grandma

Nat and the Nap

by Tamira Johnson

illustrated by Gary Undercuffler

We can see  Dad .

We can see  sit.

Dad

We can see Nat **and** 

.

Nat can nap.

 can  .

Dad yawn

Nat can see  nap.

Dad

Unit 3

Word Count: 26

Decodable Words

Target Phonics Elements: Review Consonants /m/*m*, /s/*s*, /p/*p*, /t/*t*; Short *a*
Sam, Pat

High-Frequency Words

see, the, we
Review: *can*

Word Count: 32

Decodable Words

Target Phonics Element: Short *i*
Tim

High-Frequency Words

to
Review: *can, like, see, the, we*

Word Count: 24

Decodable Words

Target Phonics Element: Initial /n/*n*
Nat, nap
Review: *sit*

High-Frequency Words

and
Review: *can, see, we*

Decoding skills taught to date:

Consonants /m/*m*, /s/*s*, /p/*p*, /t/*t*; Short *a*; Short *i*; Initial and Final /n/*n*